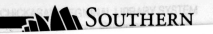 SOUTHERN

D1297997

DATE	ISSUED TO

DEMCO

SOUTH AFRICA

Ο ΦΙΛΕΛΕΙ

ΗΜΕΡΗΣΙΑ ΕΦΗΜΕΡΙΣ Ε ΤΗΝ

ΕΔΕΚ ΖΗΤΑ ΠΕΙΘΑ

τήρης Μιχαήλ

Herald INTERNATIONAL Tribu

PUBLISHED WITH THE NEW YORK TIMES AND THE WASHINGTON POST

London, Tuesday, March 8, 1994

servants
to have been too
claim immunity
ments that do not
plications for

Mr Clarke has a
signing six public
immunity certi
during his year
Home Office on se
grounds.

voys
afat
t to
Talks

e Overture
esolve Issue
nian Security

Alan Cowell
w York Times Service

With passions and blood-
h the Israeli-occu-
ael sent envoys to
e Liberation
the first
ht the
t.

Α ΚΑΙ ΘΑ ΣΥΓΚΑΛΕ

ΩΝ Ε
ΕΥΙ

• Σήμερα: Συν
• Γαλανός: Συ

Γράφει: Α.Λυκαύγης

ΙΣ σοβαρές του αν
εξελίξεις κι ενδε
ρόστσος της Δημοκρ
μβούλιο

'Cleansers' of Muslims Show No Sign of Yielding

By Roger Cohen
New York Times Service

ZVORNIK, Bosnia-Herzegovina — Up through a ghostly terrain of smashed and ransacked former Muslim homes, Branko Grujic led the way, intent on showing off his crowning contribution to what he calls the victory of Serbian Orthodox Christianity over Islam in Bosnia.

Mr. Grujic, the mayor of this northeastern Bosnian town now controlled by Serbs and completely "cleansed" of its 40,000 prewar Muslim inhabitants, has a pet project. It stands atop the escarpment that overlooks Zvornik and the meandering sweep of the Drina River.

Arriving at the summit of the cliff, Mr. Grujic paused to kiss a wooden cross he has had erected before declaring: "The Turks destroyed the Serbian church that was here when they arrived in Zvornik in 1463. Now we are rebuilding the church and reclaiming this as Serbian land forever and

There is indeed a cruel finality to

of thousands of Muslims have been pushed out by force, many of them to Bosnian government-controlled territory around Srebrenica and Tuzla.

Such activity, and the uncompromising attitude of Mr. Grujic, suggest that Serbian readiness to accept new peace proposals from the United States may be scant.

Serbs in general remain committed to holding onto land they have seized by force and

The UN deploys troops around T
in preparation for an aid

appear to have little
Bosnian politic
with Mus

"Look
point
shif

Le gouvernement israélien divisé face aux colons extrémistes

Les tractations continuent en Israël à propos de l'entrée au gouvernement du parti Tsomet du général Rafaël souhaitée par M. Rabin, site de gauche Meretz -

opposé les membres du gouvernem
mesures à prendre contre les
veille, entre 25 000 et 30 0
dont quelques milliers
à Tel-Aviv pour réc
diate des extrém
occupés, voire, po
des colons

1 PRECIO: 100 PTS.

PIDEN «DEMOCRAC

tras euro
% de m

Cli
Is

T

واشنطن خليل المعلوف:
من رفيق من راغده در
من نيويورك، من رشيد خذا
تونس، القاهرة، القدس المحت
الحياة

وصف رابين امس وجو
اسحق الخليل اجلاه
مدينة لن يطلب من
انه لن استسلام في ا
والاتصالات من ل
لجنة

موقعة

مصري

Published by Raintree Steck-Vaughn Publishers, an imprint of Steck-Vaughn Company

Designed and produced by Aladdin Books
Editor: Jen Green
Designer: Tessa Barwick
Consultant: Catherine Bradley

Raintree Steck-Vaughn Publishers staff
Project Manager: Julie Klaus
Editor: Kathy DeVico
Electronic Production: Scott Melcer

Library of Congress Cataloging-in-Publication Data
Lowis, Peter.
    South Africa, free at last / Peter Lowis.
       p.   cm. — (Topics in the news)
    "Special edition."
    Includes index.
    ISBN 0-8172-4175-2
    1. Apartheid — South Africa — Juvenile literature.
2. South Africa — Race relations — Juvenile literature.
3. South Africa — Politics and government — Juvenile literature. [1. South Africa.] I. Title. II. Series.
DT1757.L69   1996
305.8'00968—dc20   95-12096
                                 CIP
                                  AC

Printed and bound in Belgium
1 2 3 4 5 6 7 8 9 0   99 98 97 96 95

SOUTH AFRICA

Free at Last

Peter Lowis

Dawn heralds an ANC demonstration during the apartheid years.

SOUTHERN OKLAHOMA Library System
Ardmore, Oklahoma

RAINTREE STECK-VAUGHN PUBLISHERS
A Steck-Vaughn Company
Austin, Texas

Let Freedom Reign

South Africans win democracy at last

Τ he South African election of 1994 was a major milestone of the twentieth century. It marked the beginning of a peaceful and democratic society in a country torn apart by interracial conflict and political violence — a negotiated revolution.

Nelson Mandela of the ANC is South Africa's new president.

World attention focused on South Africa as the nation celebrated its very first democratic election. Now that the excitement has died down and the reporters and television crews have left, South Africa faces new challenges. Decades of racial discrimination have damaged the economy and left many thousands of people in great poverty. This book presents articles and pictures to show how South Africa is working to build a new nation out of the ruins of the old. A section on the country's history (pages 9–22) explores the background to the historic events that took place in 1994.

Supporters of the African National Congress celebrate their party's victory, in May 1994.

The Birth of a New South Africa

In April 1994, democracy was born in South Africa. For the first time, people of all races could vote for the government of their choice. The election marked the end of a long struggle against an unjust system of racial separation, called apartheid.

Apartheid reserved much of the land, the country's wealth, and the best education and jobs for a minority of South Africans who were classified as white. White people alone could vote. For most of the apartheid era, Black Africans, Indians, and people of mixed racial background, called "Coloreds," who form a majority in South Africa, had no vote.

The 1994 election showed how ordinary people can unite to overcome injustice. Nelson Mandela is just one of many individuals who risked their lives to fight against apartheid. He was imprisoned by the white minority government in 1962. During the 27 years he spent in jail, he became the world's most famous political prisoner. In 1994 he became the first president of a new, free South Africa.

Millions patiently waited in line in the blazing sun to cast their vote.

The People Shall Govern

"I have waited all my life for this day."

A new flag was raised above South Africa on April 27, 1994. It honored a new era of freedom and opened the first full day of voting in South Africa's first democratic general election.

South Africa had never before held an election on such a large scale. More than 19 million people turned out to vote. The bombs of right-wing terrorists failed to discourage them, but there were times when the process seemed threatened by organizational problems. Many people waited in line for hours, and some even waited days. Voting time was extended for an extra day to allow thousands more to vote. Despite some minor irregularities in the voting process, the election was pronounced "substantially free and fair" by international observers. South Africa's new Government of National Unity (GNU) includes perhaps the widest range of political opinion ever represented within one cabinet. Since South Africans hold very different political views, the hope is that every party will be able to negotiate an arrangement that will help to satisfy its supporters.

Government of National Unity (parties receiving less than 5% of the vote not shown)

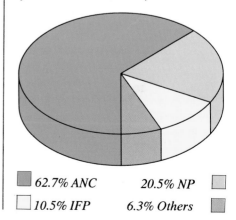

■ 62.7% ANC	20.5% NP ☐
☐ 10.5% IFP	6.3% Others ■

ANC Wins Lion's Share of the Vote

Seven political parties met for the first National Assembly on May 6, 1994. The African National Congress won a large majority. The National Party and the Inkatha Freedom Party were well represented, while Africanists, right-wingers, and Christian Democrats filled the remaining seats.

The National Party (NP) came a distant second to the ANC, winning 82 seats. Under its leader, F.W. de Klerk (below), who was the former state president, the party helped to abolish the apartheid system it had upheld for more than 40 years. The National Party succeeded in winning enough seats to secure an important role in the new government.

The Inkatha Freedom Party (IFP), which was led by Chief Buthelezi (above), won 43 seats. Most of its support came from the Zulu-speaking people in Kwazulu/Natal. The IFP favors confederalism, which gives the provinces more control over their own affairs.

The African National Congress (ANC), working in alliance with the South African Communist Party (SACP), swept to a victory in the election. Led by Nelson Mandela (above), the party took 252 seats in the National Assembly and won control of seven provincial assemblies. Since 1912, the ANC has campaigned to end the white minority rule in South Africa.

Four parties won fewer than ten seats, including the Democratic Party and the right-wing Freedom Front, campaigning for an Afrikaner homeland. The Pan-Africanist Congress campaigned for the return of lands to the African people. The African Christian Democratic Party won some support.

Sixteen million of South Africa's 40 million people live below the poverty line.

Healing the Wounds of Apartheid

Enforced racial separation created a society in which many people suffer from poverty and homelessness. To help end such hardship, the Government of National Unity has begun to carry out its Reconstruction and Development Program (RDP).

Generations of discrimination have left a great inequality in living standards among South Africans. Most of those whom apartheid was designed to benefit enjoy a high standard of living. But 16 million South Africans lack the basic necessities of housing, nutrition, and proper medical care. Less than half of African children go to school, and unemployment is very high.

The RDP plans to change South Africa into a society in which all can share the country's wealth. Its tasks include building homes, improving education, creating jobs, providing affordable medical care, and giving land to the people.

ANC Introduces Free Medical Care

Anew plan to provide affordable medical care for all is one of the first steps to be introduced under the Reconstruction and Development Program. Health minister, Dr. Nkosazana Zuma, announced that children who are under the age of six and pregnant women would be the first to qualify.

The new health plan aims to give all South Africans equal access to medicines and hospitals. During apartheid, diseases caused by malnutrition and lack of proper sanitation were common in the black townships. Medical centers there did not have enough funds to cope with the situation. The new plan places special emphasis on ending poor nutrition. In July 1994, children and pregnant women, who now qualify for free medical care, crowded into hospitals and clinics.

 Up to 3 million families homeless

 2 million children without schools

 Between 6 and 10 million unemployed

 Between 5 and 8 million live in shacks.

 10–12 million are without clean water.

 15–20 million lack adequate sanitation.

 20 million are without electricity.

Challenges facing South Africa's new government

Who Pays for the RDP?

In April 1994, the ANC estimated that the RDP will cost 39 billion Rands ($11 trillion) over five years. The ANC plans to raise funds by cutting spending on defense and other government departments. More money will be collected through new taxes, including a "wealth tax" of five percent and an increase in some other taxes. However, the RDP depends mainly upon private investment from successful businesses.

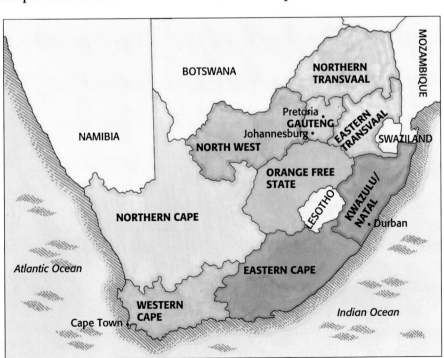

South Africa is now a unified country with nine new provinces.

Legacy of Violence

The new South Africa faces many challenges to its peace and security.

Violence between the ANC and Inkatha threatens newfound unity.

Around the time of the election, South Africa was more peaceful than it had been for years. But the conditions that produced so much violence during the apartheid era still remain. Violent crimes are common, and the threat of renewed fighting among rival groups is never very far away.

Since the 1980s, the conflict between ANC and Inkatha supporters has claimed thousands of lives (see page 21). But the recent election has brought new hope for peace. In May, South Africa's Human Rights Committee said that deaths due to political violence had fallen to their lowest level since 1991. However, crime also threatens the country's stability. Armed bank raids, muggings, and burglaries are common in a country where machine guns can be obtained illegally at a low cost.

Afrikaners Demand White Homeland

Most South Africans voted for a united country in which people of all races can live together. But the Freedom Front and the far-right Conservative Party are against this. They have demanded their own separate country within South Africa, called a volkstat (Afrikaner people's state). Many "volkstaters" are trying to achieve their aim peacefully, but some seem to prefer violence. Eugène Terre' Blanche, the leader of the racist neo-Nazi Afrikaner Resistance Movement, has threatened to start a civil war if the demands for a volkstat are not met. In June, President Mandela spoke of a vote for Afrikaners that would test their support for the idea.

Volkstaters want a homeland.

"The process of conquest from the beginning engendered wars of resistance, which in turn gave rise to our struggle for national liberation."

Generations of Struggle

The abuse of African peoples began with the arrival of the first European settlers in 1652. During the next 250 years, South Africa's kingdoms and tribal chiefdoms were gradually conquered by Europeans. By 1900, the foundations of apartheid were established. It was against this background of persecution that the struggle for liberation began.

These modern campaigners carry traditional Zulu weapons.

People known collectively as the Khoisan first moved into what is now South Africa 10,000 years ago. They lived by hunting and by gathering food from the land. The San people, once known as Bushmen, were hunter-gatherers who decorated caves with their pictures (above). Khoisan who became cattle herders moved southward into the Cape to find new grazing areas. They called themselves Khoikhoi, meaning "men of men."

The Early History

The Khoikhoi (above) were the earliest inhabitants of the Cape.

During the 1700s, the European settlement expanded in South Africa. Farms spread out from the southwestern tip, and nomadic trekboers (below) roamed hundreds of miles grazing their cattle.

In A.D. 100 people from central Africa began moving into the northeast and east of South Africa. They established settled communities that grew crops, herded cattle, and mined metals, such as iron.

Over many generations, members of tribal communities who were descendants of the people of the equatorial rain forest, drifted into southern Africa. They formed two language groups. The Nguni drove their cattle down the Indian Ocean coastline, settling in South Africa's eastern and southern regions. Their descendants include the modern Xhosa, Zulu, Ndebele, and Swazi. The Sotho and Tswana people stayed in the high central plateau of the old Transvaal province.

Khoikhoi tribespeople encountered the first Dutch settlers in 1652.

In 1652 Khoikhoi cattle herders living in South Africa's southwestern corner discovered that white Europeans had sailed into Table Bay. This is where Cape Town stands today. The Europeans built a fort and set up a supply station for the ships of the Dutch East India Company. These ships made many trading voyages to the Far East. Within five years, the Dutch station had become a permanent settlement. Some of the settlers started farms on lands that the Khoikhoi had occupied for centuries. In 1659 the Dutch farmers, called Boers, fought the Khoikhoi for control of the land. Armed with better weapons, the Boers expanded their farms. Unable to fight off European diseases, the Khoikhoi eventually all died.

Under King Shaka, who reigned from 1818 to 1828, the small Zulu clan grew into a powerful nation. In the 1820s, thousands of Africans fled from Shaka's army.

The Boers' migration became known as the Great Trek.

King Cetshwayo ruled the Zulu from 1873 to 1884. His warriors won important battles against the British Army during the Anglo-Zulu Wars of the 1870s.

The British seized Cape Colony from the Dutch in 1806, which strengthened their trade links with the East. The British army waged war against the Xhosa and other African peoples throughout the 1800s. Meanwhile, thousands of Africans were driven inland by the advances of a mighty Zulu army led by King Shaka. The Ndebele built a powerful empire as they moved north from Zululand.

In 1834 slavery was abolished throughout the British Empire. Angered by this and resentful of British control over the Cape, the Boers began a great migration into the interior. In the 1850s, some 6,000 of these travelers set up two Boer Republics, the Orange Free State (OFS) and the Transvaal, or South African Republic (ZAR).

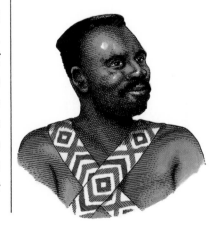

The European Domination

The scramble for South Africa's wealth and land

In 1870 the Boer and British governments conducted a series of campaigns against the Xhosa, Zulu, Venda, and other peoples. By 1900, almost nine-tenths of what is now South Africa was in European hands.

In the late 1800s, diamonds and gold were discovered in the Boer republics. The deposits were soon in the hands of large companies that needed huge numbers of laborers to work the deep-level mines.

Although Africans had lost control of much of the country, many still lived by farming and were able to provide for themselves. But now a new hut tax forced Africans to pay money to the government for their homes, even if these homes stood on land they had occupied for centuries. Since most of these people did not possess western money, they were forced to work for white employers. As more and more workers left their villages, family life broke down, crop yields decreased, and poverty increased. This was the beginning of South Africa's migrant labor system, which would continue later under apartheid law.

Zulu warriors defeated the

The discovery of gold and diamonds in 1866–1867 sparked economic change. New laws forced thousands of Africans into the mines. There they worked under terrible conditions for low pay. At this time, laborers were also imported from India to work in plantations and factories in Natal.

The discovery of gold caused another conflict—the Anglo-Boer War (1899–1902). Eager to win control of the gold-rich Boer Republics, Great Britain tried to seize the Orange Free State and the Transvaal. The Boers began a guerrilla war to preserve their independence, but in the end suffered defeat.

The Boers fought against Great Britain from 1899 to 1902.

British at Isandhlwana in 1879.

In 1906 the Zulu chief Bambatha led a rebellion against British rule. The British army responded by killing almost 4,000 resisters. A century after it had seized the Cape, Great Britain crushed the last armed African rebellion.

In 1910 the British colonies in Natal and the Cape joined together with the defeated Boer republics to form the Union of South Africa. The union did not recognize the rights of South Africa's black majority. The Natives Land Act of 1913 made the land seizures of the previous century legal. It prohibited Africans from buying land in all but 13 percent of South Africa, reserving the rest of the country for whites.

The South African Native National Congress was founded in 1912 to unite Africans in the new era of white domination. The Reverend John Dube (left) was its first president. In 1914 Dube led a delegation to try to persuade Great Britain to stop the 1913 Land Act.

Sol T. Plaatje was a founding member of the ANC. He started a campaigning newspaper in 1901. The ANC had initially hoped to end discrimination through the force of reason. Plaatje toured Great Britain and North America, giving talks about the troubles of black South Africans.

Apartheid and Defiance

Jan Smuts led the United Party from 1919 to 1924 and 1939 to 1948. During World War II, it seemed hopeful that he could bring more rights to Africans.

But Smuts was defeated in the 1948 election.

Chief Albert Luthuli was ANC president between 1952 and 1960. He won the 1961 Nobel Peace Prize for his admirable work against apartheid.

During the 1920s and 1930s, the South African Native National Congress, now the African National Congress (ANC) gained an increasing amount of support. In 1948 racist policies in South Africa became law in the apartheid system.

The 1923 Native Urban Areas Act stated that the number of black Africans living in towns would be controlled, and that blacks should live in separate areas from the whites. In 1948 the United Party was defeated by the National Party (NP), led by D.F. Malan. The NP tried to advance the interests of Afrikaners (as the Boers were called) without regard for South Africa's black majority.

Police move in to disperse women protesters near Durban in 1959.

The new government passed six laws to form the basis of a system of enforced racial separation — apartheid. The 1950 Population Registration Act labeled all South Africans as belonging to one of four racial groups: Blacks, Whites, Indians, and Coloreds. A person's race grouping affected every aspect of his or her life; for example, place of residence, education, type of work, and freedom of movement. The 1952 Pass Laws required black Africans to carry a pass (identity card). They could be arrested for failing to show one. The ANC started a campaign of mass action against apartheid in 1952.

Born in 1918, Nelson Mandela was trained as a lawyer. He led the ANC Youth League in the 1950s. After Sharpeville, he went into hiding to organize armed resistance against the government.

Sharpeville, 1960. Police shot many in the back as they ran away.

The campaign brought thousands together to break the new laws. Many were arrested and imprisoned, but the ANC won thousands of new supporters.

In 1955 the ANC and its allies formed the Congress Alliance. Around 3,000 activists from all races wrote the Freedom Charter (shown right). The NP condemned the charter and charged 156 Congress leaders with treason.

On March 21, 1960, a crowd gathered in Sharpeville, Transvaal, to demonstrate against the Pass Laws. The police opened fire, killing 69 protesters. The incident was a turning point. Across the country, there were demonstrations to inform others of the mass murder. Within two weeks, the ANC and the members who broke away from Pan-Africanist Congress (PAC) were banned.

THE FREEDOM CHARTER

- *The people shall govern.*
- *All national groups shall have equal rights.*
- *The people shall share in the country's wealth.*
- *The land shall be shared among those who work it.*
- *All people shall be equal before the law.*
- *All shall enjoy equal human rights.*
- *There shall be work and security.*
- *The doors of learning and culture shall be opened.*
- *There shall be houses, security, and comfort.*
- *There shall be peace and friendship.*

"The time comes in the life of any nation when there remain only two choices: submit or fight. That time has now come to South Africa."

The Clampdown

H.F. Verwoerd was "the grand architect of apartheid." His Bantustan policy denied citizenship to black South Africans, by making them citizens of the homelands.

Oliver Tambo served as president of the ANC from 1960 to 1991. He helped build international opposition to apartheid.

As Nelson Mandela said, "50 years of non-violence had brought the Africans nothing."

With all means of peaceful protest closed to them, the ANC and PAC began to organize armed resistance against the government. In 1961 the ANC and the South African Communist Party (SACP) created a new military force, called Umkhonto we Sizwe (Spear of the Nation, otherwise known as MK). Nelson Mandela became its first commander.

In the 1960s, MK launched a series of attacks, bombing government targets. Mandela was arrested in 1962. Later that year, the United Nations voted sanctions (bans on international trade) against South Africa. In 1964 Mandela and seven other MK leaders were sentenced to life in prison. With its leaders in prison, the resistance movement inside South Africa was crushed. Led by Oliver Tambo, the ANC continued its struggle in exile, from headquarters in Zambia. In the 1960s and 1970s, the NP, under H.F. Verwoerd, introduced its Bantustan policy. It divided the land reserved for black Africans into ten homelands, or "bantustans."

In Soweto, in 1976, police opened

TOWNSHIP RESIDENT, 1976:

"When your kids are shot, you cannot keep your cool. I saw people fleeing in panic and shot as they were running away."

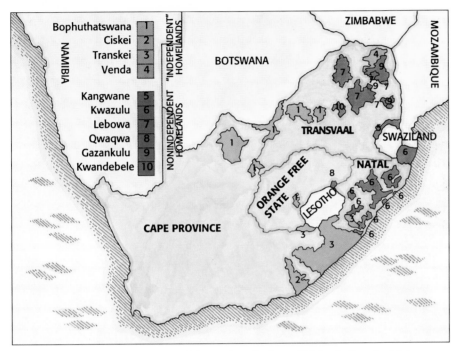

Bophuthatswana	1	"INDEPENDENT" HOMELANDS
Ciskei	2	
Transkei	3	
Venda	4	
Kangwane	5	NONINDEPENDENT HOMELANDS
Kwazulu	6	
Lebowa	7	
Qwaqwa	8	
Gazankulu	9	
Kwandebele	10	

NAMIBIA — BOTSWANA — ZIMBABWE — MOZAMBIQUE — TRANSVAAL — SWAZILAND — NATAL — ORANGE FREE STATE — LESOTHO — CAPE PROVINCE

Bantustans: Ten scattered homelands for all black South Africans

fire on unarmed protesters.

The Bantustan plan forced millions of black people from their homes. Many were sent to places where there were no buildings and no jobs.

The tide began to turn against apartheid on June 16, 1976. In the township of Soweto, thousands of young people marched against government-imposed changes in schooling. One change meant that half their lessons would be in Afrikaans, a language similar to Dutch. Police opened fire on the protest. Across the country, township residents rose up against apartheid on a larger scale than ever before.

Stephen Bantu Biko, born in 1946, was a leader of the Black Consciousness Movement in the 1970s. The movement stressed pride in being black. As a student, Biko came to believe that white-dominated political groups could never win the fight against apartheid. In 1968 he helped to found the South African Students Organization (SASO), and became its first president. Biko was banned by the government in 1973. Police arrested him many times, but never actually charged him with a crime. Biko died in 1977, while in police custody. A doctor's report showed that he had received massive blows to the head while in jail. His death inspired thousands in the struggle against apartheid.

Life Under Apartheid

Enforced racial separation was part of everyday life in South Africa. In its mildest forms, it caused inconvenience. At its worst, it brought poverty and death.

A domestic servant looks after her employer's children in a whites-only suburb. Under apartheid, people of different racial groups had to live in separate areas. But many white families employed nonwhite workers as low-paid servants who lived with them for most of the week. Some black nannies could spend little time with their own children.

During apartheid, many black workers lived outside of the homelands, in townships near cities reserved for whites. Illegal camps formed. This camp, called Crossroads, was raided by bands of "white-scarves," connected with government security forces. Here a Crossroads resident throws water on the remains of her home after a raid.

A typical railroad station during the years of apartheid had separate sections for black and white people. After 1948, "whites only" signs went up to enforce apartheid rules. These signs kept black and white South Africans separate in doctors' waiting rooms, public toilets, on buses and trains, park benches, and even beaches.

A man is arrested for not obeying apartheid laws. Over the years, opposition to apartheid grew. The government responded with even more strict laws. Hundreds of thousands were arrested for "crimes," ranging from not having an identity card to acts of protest. Many were young people under 16, especially after 1976. Some prisoners were tortured while in police custody.

State of Emergency

President P.W. Botha wanted to put an end to support for the ANC in black-ruled countries neighboring South Africa. So he sent out government troops on raids to scare them.

ANC leader, Walter Sisulu, was imprisoned for life in 1964. He was freed in 1989 and became ANC deputy president in 1991.

By the mid-1980s, apartheid was in crisis.

In August 1983, 575 different organizations who represented workers, women, youths, and churches met in Cape Town to form the United Democratic Front (UDF). Building on the work of the ANC, the UDF organized numerous boycotts, strikes, and other protests against apartheid. In 1984 the longest, strongest, and most dedicated fight against white rule began.

Residents of Soweto faced police rifles at a demonstration in 1980.

In exile, the ANC had called for a campaign to make the townships "ungovernable." The uprising spread across South Africa. In response, the government declared a state of emergency. This gave the police and army new powers to arrest people. The uprising lasted for three years. More than 3,000 people lost their lives in the conflict, and 30,000 were imprisoned. Workers formed the Congress of South African Trade Unions (COSATU) in 1985. Allied to the UDF, it became a powerful force to fight apartheid.

People rebuilt their homes after their camp was attacked in 1986.

Winnie Mandela fought for the release of her husband. She soon came to symbolize challenge to white rule.

Chief Buthelezi, president of the Inkatha Freedom Party (IFP), condemned the UDF as "a force for disunity." During 1975, he attracted many Zulu-speaking people to the IFP. In 1984 a bloody conflict between IFP and ANC supporters took hundreds of lives.

By the late 1980s, opposition to apartheid had reached its peak. Since the 1970s, South Africa had waged undeclared war on many of its neighbors to keep the enemies of apartheid from organizing. But in 1988, Angola and its allies defeated the invading South African army. Facing disaster from international sanctions, the government realized that it had to settle its differences with the black majority in South Africa.

F. W. de Klerk succeeded Botha as president in 1989. In February 1990, he announced the lifting of the bans on the ANC, PAC, and SACP. "The time for negotiation has come," he said. Nine days later, Mandela walked free from prison.

Nelson Mandela, freed in 1990.

Archbishop Desmond Tutu has spoken out against injustice all his life. He became an Anglican priest in 1961. In 1984 he won the Nobel Peace Prize for his work against apartheid.

The End of Apartheid

Chief Buthelezi was the leader of the Kwazulu homeland. He refused to join in talks with the ANC and NP in 1992. His Inkatha Party entered the 1994 election just seven days before voting began.

F.W. de Klerk was a major force in ending apartheid. In 1993 he shared the Nobel Peace Prize with Mandela.

In 1990 the ANC announced the end of its armed struggle against apartheid. In 1991 the National Party began to talk with political opponents and homeland governments about the future of South Africa. F. W. de Klerk announced plans for a nonracial government to replace the white minority rule.

In 1993 ANC supporters were angered by the murder of leader, Chris Hani.

In 1991 the last apartheid laws were suspended. Some sanctions were lifted, though black people could not yet vote. Talks continued for the next two years, though there were times when violence threatened to destroy the chance of peaceful change. In late 1993, negotiators managed to set an election date. Their achievement was "a negotiated revolution"— the first one in history.

Workers display South Africa's new flag (shown here upside down).

Blueprint for the New South Africa

Following the success of the 1994 election, one of the most important tasks for the government was to write a new constitution for South Africa. The constitution will map out how the government will work and what rights each citizen will have.

On November 17, 1993, the NP and ANC accepted a new constitution. It was the first time in South Africa's history that the law recognized all people, black and white, as being equal. But the new constitution is only a short-term solution, intended to last for a limited time. Over the next two years, parliament must draw up a final constitution. It will cover democracy, human rights, and specify the powers that each province will have to govern its own affairs.

Building a Nonsexist South Africa

At his inauguration, President Mandela promised to build a nonsexist South Africa, in which no people are treated unfairly because they are male or female. South Africa has been a male-dominated country, but things are changing. The new National Assembly has one of the highest proportions of women of any parliament. Out of 400 members, 106 are women, and two of them are senior ministers. But women leaders say it will be a "long, hard fight" to overcome discrimination. Women form 53 percent of South Africa's population, but the majority are poor and cannot read or write.

Women laborers dig up a Soweto road.

People who live in these settlements have to make shelters out of whatever materials they can find.

Housing the Homeless

There is a housing crisis in South Africa today. About three million people are homeless, and up to eight million live in shacks and camps. In order to meet the housing demands of its growing population, South Africa must build more than 300,000 new homes each year until the year 2004.

Living conditions remain poor in many townships that were formerly set aside for black people. Residents live in shacks, with little or no lighting and poor sewage facilities.

The ANC's Bill of Rights states that all South Africans have a right to a secure place in which to live. This promise will cost nearly R9 billion ($2.4 trillion) a year, over half of which must come from private businesses and foreign aid.

In July 1994, workers at Kutlwanong in the Orange Free State began building the first "RDP home," one of 747 intended for a community of mine workers and their families. The local community, the mining company, and the government are all funding the project. Plans like this will provide a million new jobs a year.

Reclaiming the Land

Life is hard for small-scale farmers who had their land taken away.

By the time apartheid ended, more than three million black South Africans had been removed and sent to overcrowded homelands and townships. Many small-scale farmers had also been sent away from their lands.

In 1994 the Government of National Unity started a national land reform program. The program was designed to ease some of the hardships caused by the policies of the apartheid years.

The program is based on two basic policies. Land restitution enables families to reclaim lands that were taken away from them under unfair laws, such as the 1913 Land Act. The second policy, land redistribution, proposes sharing the land among all South Africans in a fairer and more equal way. This policy will work to provide affordable land for the poor and will also make full use of any unoccupied land.

UNEQUAL SHARES

South Africa has the extremes of poverty and wealth. The vast majority of the people who are poor and landless today were classified as black under the apartheid system. Much of the land and money remains in white hands.

■ *Black*   *Indian* ■
□ *White*   *Colored* ▨

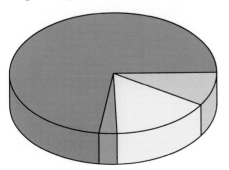

Population at the end of apartheid

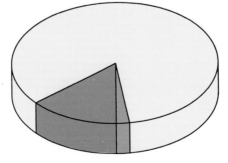

Land distribution

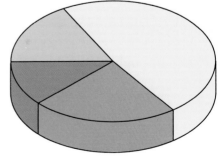

Income distribution

Let There Be Work

The RDP will create new jobs outside of the mines.

At least six million South Africans are without work. But some say the true figure could be as high as 21 million, or half the population. Until the RDP creates new jobs, this number is likely to rise. For every 100 young people who entered the job market in 1993, only six of them found work.

South Africa's new government plans to create thousands of jobs through national public works programs. These will try to build homes, repair environmental damage, and provide electricity and clean water to underdeveloped areas. About two-thirds of working people lack the skills they need because they were not given opportunities for training during the apartheid years. South Africa is now working to make education and training available to everyone.

Education for All

South Africa is now working to provide equal educational opportunities for all its people, regardless of race, sex, age, or language. On January 1, 1995, school attendance became a requirement for all children for the first time. The new government will try to provide ten years of free education to every South African child up to the age of 15. In order to meet this demand, many new schools must be built.

Under apartheid, children who were classified as black

Township schools are crowded,

were not given a proper education. This was an attempt by the government to make sure that black children remained a source of cheap, unskilled labor for whites. By 1994, apartheid had left nearly two million black children without schools to attend. In some townships and rural areas, the community schools tried to fill the gap but failed. Andile, a student who has no real school, reports: "Our classrooms are ship containers, [with] no furniture, stationery, reading, or textbooks. Teachers at our school don't get paid."

It is not safe for children to play outside because of all the violence.

Back to School

New Hope for South Africa's
"Lost Generation"

The many uprisings of the 1980s disrupted the education of a whole generation of township youth, who experienced instead the hardship and violence of the apartheid conflict. This generation of young people are sometimes known as "the Lost Generation" because of their misfortune.

In a country with at least six million unemployed, the young adults of "the Lost Generation" urgently need education and skills. To help ease the problem, the RDP has plans for Adult Basic Education (ABE). Through ABE, every adult who was denied proper schooling as a child will have the opportunity to gain what is considered the equivalent of a secondary school education. The RDP also includes plans to make sure that employers do not overlook these young people.

and have few textbooks.

World Welcomes New Democracy

In May 1994, the largest gathering of heads of state ever to attend an inauguration watched Nelson Mandela take the oath as president. For more than 30 years, South Africa's apartheid policies had made it "the skunk of the world." Now it could take its place in the international community.

World reaction to the recent developments in South Africa has been positively joyful. People in many countries see the defeat of apartheid as a major victory in the worldwide struggle for human rights. United States Congressman Dellums, who represented African Americans at Mandela's inauguration, said: "As I watched Nelson Mandela raise his hand, I cried great tears of joy. I saw an incredible force being unleashed that will go far beyond South Africa. It says to us that if our cause is just...some day we will prevail."

During the apartheid era, people all over the world refused to buy goods, such as wines and fruit, that are exported from South Africa.

International Sanctions Lifted

In October 1993, Nelson Mandela addressed the United Nations. He called for the lifting of sanctions that had restricted trade with South Africa during the apartheid years, on the grounds that South Africa was in the process of becoming a democracy. Sanctions had included a ban on South Africa's participation in official sports events. In 1993 the international community welcomed the return of South Africa at such events as the World Athletic Championships.

On June 1, 1994, South Africa rejoined the British Commonwealth of Nations. Then on June 23, the republic took its seat at the United Nations for the first time in 20 years. The country had been banned from the UN in 1974, as part of the protest against apartheid.

South Africa's rugby team in action in 1994

South Africa Seeks New Trading Links

Trade in advanced weaponry systems will help fund the RDP.

South Africa needs money from foreign countries. Some funds have already been donated. Japan announced an aid package of $1.3 billion. In the long run, South Africa must meet its needs through international trade. Since the 1800s, mining has formed the basis of the economy. During apartheid, the country built a successful arms industry. South Africa has recently signed a $120 million contract to provide weapons to Oman in the Middle East.

South Africa Rejoins Its African Family

For more than 30 years, Africa shunned South Africa. But in May 1994, South Africa took its seat at the Organization of African Unity (OAU). "Welcome to your African family," said the OAU secretary-general. South Africa is building a new role for itself on the continent. In June, it sent a field hospital to treat refugees from war-torn Rwanda. In July, it helped the leaders of Angola and Zaire reach an agreement on a meeting to end the 19-year-old Angolan war.

South Africa attends the OAU in 1994.

In the new South Africa, all races have equal political power.

A Rainbow Nation

A vision for South Africa's future

In his acceptance speech, President Mandela promised: "We shall build the society in which all South Africans, both black and white, will be able to walk tall, without any fear in their hearts...a rainbow nation at peace with itself and the world."

Nelson Mandela's vision presents a huge challenge. The election brought equal political power to black South Africans for the first time since European settlement began. But money, land, and big business remain largely in the hands of white South Africans. In a country where so many have so little, such vast differences in wealth are a threat to peace. The achievement of democracy has brought with it new hope for nonviolent change. The recent election has been described as a "miracle." But in the months to come, South Africa must attempt yet another miracle — to build a strong, nonracial society and, at the same time, try to accommodate groups such as the right-wing "volkstaters," who seek self-rule outside of a unified South African state.

The Struggle Continues

As election excitement died down, new difficulties arose in South Africa. The first conflict between the old authorities and the new government erupted when the white-controlled Johannesburg city council demolished 800 shacks in a camp. In mid-1994, striking workers demanded better pay and working conditions. South Africa must also tackle the problems of crime and violence. Many challenges lie ahead if the government is to fulfill its promises and achieve harmony among the very different peoples it represents.

Archbishop Tutu joins celebrations for the new South Africa.

CHRONOLOGY

8000s B.C. Khoisan peoples entered South Africa.

A.D. 100s Nguni, Tswana, and Sotho people began moving in from the north.

1652 Dutch settlers arrived at the Cape.

1806 Great Britain took over the Cape Colony.

1820s King Shaka's army waged war.

1836 Boers began their Great Trek from the Cape.

1870–1880 African kingdoms were crushed by British and Boer armies.

1880–1881, 1899–1902 Anglo-Boer Wars

1906 Bambatha rebellion

1910 British colonies and Boer republics established the Union of South Africa.

1912 Founding of the ANC

1913 The Natives Land Act was passed.

1948 The National Party (NP) won the election. Apartheid became official.

1952 ANC began a Defiance Campaign.

1955 The Congress of the People wrote and adopted the Freedom Charter.

1956 To protest against the Pass Laws, 20,000 women marched to the government buildings in Pretoria.

1956–1961 156 Congress leaders stood trial for treason.

1959 PAC formed.

1960 Police shot 69 protesters in Sharpeville. The ANC and PAC were banned.

1961 Umkhonto we Sizwe, otherwise known as MK, began its armed struggle.

1962 Police arrested Nelson Mandela.

1964 Nelson Mandela and other leaders were sentenced to life in prison.

1976 Soweto Uprising

1977 Death of Steve Biko

1983 United Democratic Front (UDF) formed.

1984 A countrywide uprising against apartheid began. State of emergency was declared.

1988 South African army defeated by Angola's allies

1990 President F. W. de Klerk lifted the ban on the ANC and 33 other groups. Mandela was freed after 27 years.

1991 Apartheid was abolished. CODESA talks began.

1993 Chris Hani was assassinated. Mandela and de Klerk won the Nobel Peace Prize.

1994 The ANC won the first democratic election. Mandela became president.

Photo Credits
All the pictures in this book were supplied by Frank Spooner Pictures, except pages: 2: Simon Townsley; 10: The Mansell Collection; 11: Royal Geographical Society /Bridgeman Art Library; 12–13: National Army Museum/ Bridgeman Art Library; 13: Afrikaner Museum Johannesburg /Bridgeman Art Library; 14,15: Hulton Deutsch; 19 (top): Topham Picture Point; 28 (top): Roger Vlitos; 28 (bottom): Reuters /Hulton Deutsch.

Ο ΦΙΛΕΛΕΙ

ΗΜΕΡΗΣΙΑ ΕΦΗΜΕΡΙΣ

ΕΔΕΚ ΖΗΤΑ ΠΕΙΘΑ

Herald INTERNATIONAL Tribu

PUBLISHED WITH THE NEW YORK TIMES AND THE WASHINGTON POST

London, Tuesday, March 8, 1994

'Cleansers' of Muslims Show No Sign of Yielding

By Roger Cohen
New York Times Service

ZVORNIK, Bosnia-Herzegovina — Up through a ghostly terrain of smashed and ransacked former Muslim homes, Branko Grujic led the way, intent on showing off his crowning contribution to what he calls the victory of Serbian Orthodox Christianity over Islam in Bosnia.

Mr. Grujic, the mayor of this northeastern Bosnian town now controlled by Serbs and completely "cleansed" of its 40,000 prewar Muslim inhabitants, has a pet project. It stands atop the escarpment that overlooks Zvornik and the meandering sweep of the Drina River.

Arriving at the summit of the cliff, Mr. Grujic paused to kiss a wooden cross he had erected before declaring: "The Turks destroyed the Serbian church that was here when they arrived in Zvornik in 1463. Now we are rebuilding the church and reclaiming this as Serbian land forever and

There is indeed a cruel finality to

of thousands of Muslims have been pushed out by force, many of them to Bosnian government-controlled territory around Srebrenica and Tuzla.

Such activity, and the uncompromising attitude of Mr. Grujic, suggest that Serbian readiness to accept new peace proposals from the United States may be scant.

Serbs in general remain committed to holding onto land they have seized by force and

The UN deploys troops around T in preparation for an aid

appear to have little
Bosnian politic
with Mu

"Look
poin
shif

Α ΚΑΙ ΘΑ ΣΥΓΚΑΛ

ΟΝ

ΕΥ

Σήμερα: Συ
Γαλανός: Σ

Γράφει: Α. Λυκαύγης

Τ ΙΣ σοβαρές του αν
εξελίξεις κι ενδ
ρόστκος της Δημοκρ
Συμβούλι

موقوتة

Le gouvernement israélien divisé face aux colons extrémistes

opposé les membres du gouvernem
mesures à prendre contre les
veille, entre 25 000 et 30 0
dont quelques milliers
à Tel-Aviv pour réc
diate des extrémi
occupés, voire, po
des colons

Les tractations continuent en Israël à propos de l'entrée au gouvernement du parti Tsomet du général Rafaël souhaitée par M. Rabin, gauche Meretz Shass, qui
dernier.

PIDEN «DEMOCRAC

1 PRECIO: 100 PTS.

voys
afat
t to
Talks

e Overture
esolve Issue
inian Security

J. Alan Cowell
w York Times Service

ith passions and blood-
h the Israeli-occu-
ael sent envoys to
e Liberation
the first
ht the
t.